This wonderful book belongs to:

_____

Follow the QR code or use the link to grab a **FREE PDF copy** of the fantastic '*Zen Doodles Most Popular Coloring Book*' with pages from 20 of our most popular books!

https://bit.ly/ZenDoodlesBooks

40 Elegant Sailing Ships

ADULT COLORING BOOK

Enjoy the 40 detailed drawings of sailing ships contained within this book, which are ideal for relaxation and stress relief.

We hope you enjoy completing this book. You can find other great colouring books by Zen Doodles at the following author link:

https://www.amazon.com/author/zendoodles

Thank you so much for purchasing this book!

As a small indie publisher every sale makes a huge difference, helping us create more quality books for you to enjoy.

We really hope this book has been enjoyable for you to color. If you have a minute, it would mean the world to us to hear your honest feedback by **leaving a review on Amazon.**

It does wonders for the book and we love receiving your feedback because it helps us create more of what you love!

Thanks again - the *Zen Doodles Team*

Made in the USA
Columbia, SC
07 October 2024

43762034R00046